3rd Tuesdays
Volume 1

Dylan Garcia

Copyright © 2024 by Dylan Garcia

All rights reserved.

No portion of this book may be reproduced in any form without written permission from the publisher or author, except as permitted by U.S. copyright law.

Also by Dylan Garcia

Not Every Word A Fist

Contents

About 3rd Tuesdays

A poetry slam is a competitive art form where poems are read in front of an audience. Judges are selected from the audience, and they assign scores to each poem from 1-10. 30 is the highest score a poem can achieve. Poets who receive the highest scores move to the next round.

Since 2015 Rockford, Illinois has hosted a poetry slam and open mic on the third Tuesday of each month. I have regularly attended this event and competed in the poetry slam. This is a collection of poems that I performed at this slam between the years 2015 and 2018.

The Alcoholic Considers Another Round

When I walk into this bar
Beer is waiting for me,
sweating in anticipation of my arrival.
Beer is my favorite drinking partner.
It doesn't ask questions.
It's always ready for another round.
With every sip it reminds me
alcoholism runs in my veins,
and if I cut myself open right now,
I wouldn't find even four days sober.

I sit down and watch a woman at the end of the bar
try to flirt her way into a cocktail.
She looks just like my mother,
the tangled parachute of my most vulnerable years
that sent me into free fall.
Beer notices, says,
"Your mother is a busted lighthouse.
She's the crooked compass
on the map of your homeland."

I take a drink.
Beer is correct,
yet I come here to prove my mother right.
I am worth forgetting.

Beer doesn't like when I get sad,
but one side of my family tree contains branches
made heavy by alcohol abuse.
The other side sees things that aren't actually there.
I am a convergence of battered roots.

And my grandmother once said she doesn't drink
because she's afraid she'll end up like her father.
She said a life of sobriety was better
than whatever monster she thought she'd become.
I still haven't gotten the guts to ask her
what she sees in me.

Beer tells me to ignore these stories,
says family history is what you make of it.
"Nothing wrong with a few drinks.
Nothing wrong with wanting to swallow that pain.
You've already redefined the word 'home'
to be nothing more than the cracked vinyl of a bar stool.
What would sobriety leave you to gain?"

I swiftly finish my drink,
the guilty aftertaste burning my tongue.
Beer hasn't seen my family photos, though.
I look exactly like my grandmother's fear.

The Diagnosis (Runs In The Family)

For years I've offered myself up,
a body to be possessed,
not knowing that demons
have always lived inside me.
Genetic predisposition, they call it.
Some things just run in the family.
Like secrets and fear.

I know how easy it would be
to walk into a busy street without looking.
When I try to tell my friends about this,
they don't hear the way my voice cracks
with the same sound of my great-grandfather
choking on his cries for help.

I know shame is a friend of darkness,
and silence is never golden.
It's a waiting bridge that knows my name
and wants me to come home
to the turbulent waves.

When I finally learn about my great-grandfather's suicide,
it's too late to take back my scars,
but I bet his hands could've read my skin's Braille perfectly.
We've all got our ugly,
even if we have to uproot our comfort to see it,
even if we can't call it by name.

I've learned that the greatest act of violence against myself
is putting on the mask of perfection.

When I learn about my grandmother's antidepressants
I feel like a rusted wish at the bottom of a well.
I understand now that I'm afraid of heights
because every breath on the edge of a cliff
is a fight against the urge to jump.

I didn't realize so many people in my family
were unsung survival stories.
I didn't realize the breakdown was the truth
we're all too afraid to tell.
I didn't realize Shame was so close to all of us.
We never pull him up a chair at the dinner table
with all the spotless plates.
We never answer the door when he comes home.
We can't even look him in the face.

Casualties

My uncle was born in Mexico.
As a young man he came to the United States,
joined the Marines,
took part in Desert Storm,
and learned love of this new country
while carrying a rifle.
My uncle is no longer young,
but he sleeps with the lights on.

He doesn't talk much now.
When he does speak,
it's with a mouth full of grenade,
all blood and nightmare landscapes
he refuses to describe once he comes home.

My uncle says he fought in Vietnam.
My uncle says he is the reincarnation
of a soldier who died in the jungles.
In the jungle that is his own mind
he is familiar with the smell of napalm,
rough calluses on smooth triggers,
the cries of people whose language he does not speak.

My uncle says he killed a man in Vietnam.
He uses words like M14, Huey, Howitzer,
rolls them around in his mouth like a slow mantra
like any good Marine would.

When he gives voice to his delusions
he never says PTSD.
He never admits he joined the Marines
to make America proud,
never puts into words what it felt like
to have his father pull him out by his Mexican roots
so one day he'd be told to sing death
to the tune of Red, White, Blue.

My uncle is online at two a.m. when he tells me
he doesn't sleep because
the shattered bodies from the desert
storm into his dreams.
He says,
"Those people, they never stood a chance."

I ask my uncle if he's ever heard the word "imperialism".
He says nothing.
Then he asks me if I believe in ghosts.
I say yes.
Looking at him,
the proof is undeniable.

Borderline Speaks

I'm the illness no one talks about,
the confusion caused by people
whose language only includes the words
"depression" and "bipolar".

I'm the reason your scars bloomed
in the field of your pale skin,
the reason every time you try
to say "I love you"
it comes out more like a choked last word.

I'm the reason she left you,
he left you, they all left you.
Why can't you get angry
like a normal person?
Why do you yell at people
when you need them to stay?

Don't look at me like that.

I'm just an apology you kept inside
until it expired.
I'm just the box cutter
you tell your boss you're afraid of,
the memory of trying to take your life
in a public bathroom.

I said don't look at me like that!

You're the one sitting in your apartment
nursing your guilt with a bottle of wine.
But damn it.
Some days you're so brave.

I saw the way you smiled at work
when that woman asked you
about the lipstick clutched in her hand.
Moments earlier you had been in the bathroom
drowning in your own grief.
Your eyes weren't even dry yet,
but she looked at you said,
"I feel so protective of young people.
You are the future."

I'm not saying I have all the answers.
I don't. That's why I'm always screaming,
trying to force these demons from my throat
before they manifest as another cruel word
I can't take back.

When that woman at the store
said you were the future,
do you think she saw the ghosts
of every mistake you've made?
How they haunt you like you're a lonely highway?
How they make you so difficult to navigate?

This isn't an excuse.
I'm not asking to be let off the hook.
I know my "sorry" needs to toughen up.
I just need to be reminded that
I can make things better.
I have been making things better.

Don't give up on me yet.

21 Grams

In the early 1900s,
a doctor named Duncan MacDougall,
conducted an experiment on tuberculosis patients.
During this experiment
MacDougall weighed the bodies
just before and at the moment of death.
This led the doctor to believe that
a human soul weighs twenty one grams.

The Addict mutters goodbye to his memories,
parceled out in grams of blow,
recollections dripping into a wet spot on the floor
smeared with Jameson
just as the sun peeks its head over the horizon.

The Addict sleeps for 72 hours straight
as the sun rises and sets,
rises and sets, rises and sets
and curls its lips around the face of the world
that keeps on moving while he crashes and burns.

He misses 7 calls, 26 text messages.
His phone blinks, blinks, blinks.
The Addict's heart beats and beats and beats...

Until it stops...

My Queerness Walks Into A Bar

after Franny Choi

My queerness walks into
the only gay bar in the city,
but it's Pride month,
so it's filled with unfamiliar faces.
My queerness notices a woman he's never seen before.
He says hello with a smile,
but the woman wrinkles her nose at him.
My queerness is unfazed.

As he goes to take a seat he overhears two white men
speaking about a Black man on the dance floor
with tongues that sound
like the sharpening of a guillotine.

"What you're saying is racist," my queerness says.
The two men snap to attention,
as if they'd been called by name.
"What business of yours is this?" one asks.
My queerness shifts his weight.
"Racism within the queer community is my business.
You need to stop."

My queerness gets asked to leave the bar,
is told he is causing a disruption,
is told that all these nice patrons
want to enjoy their drinks without drama.

My queerness leaves with a back turned
on a place he thought he could feel safe in.
He knows there is no pride in bigotry.

The day I started writing this poem in June of 2017,
Charleena Lyles, a pregnant black woman
and mother of four,
was murdered by two white police officers.
And while the days of Pride month tick away
I see how whitewashed this month is.
History knows well how to erase the work
done by trans women of color.

How often do people need to be reminded that
the victims of the Pulse Nightclub massacre
were largely people of color?

This month I know how many people will have a few drinks
and quietly ignore all the white queer people
who trade their rainbow flags for Confederate ones
the moment the parade ends.

My queerness only came here for a drink.
He leaves knowing there's so much work to be done.

Disarm The Resurrection

Ex-lovers, like bad dreams,
always seem to find a way to resurrect
into repeating images of flesh and dirt,
vodka and bad decisions.

When your ex comes back from the dead,
busts out from under the pile of dirt
he buried himself under
in your graveyard heart,
do not panic.

You have prepared yourself for this.
Make a circle of salt around your chair.
Remind yourself
you named that relationship devastation for a reason.
Remind yourself
how your life had progressed
in the years of his crypt-like silence.

When you see his name in your Facebook messages,
summon spirits. Take a shot for old times' sake.
When the room spins
and his ghost creeps out of the shadows
wanting to communicate,
remind yourself this is what the Quija board is for.

Put the planchette down,
ask a question to the abyss,
wait only a brief moment,
then close the board by saying
GOODBYE.

Self-Harm Is Not Love

Since the day I started writing,
people have asked me if I do love poems
knowing full well this mouth
gives birth to trauma that grows on page.

"I don't know what love is," I respond.
I can talk about what love is not.
I can talk about the identities I've mistaken for love.
I can quote sonnets,
but how do I know when love actually arrives?

My last partner was a house fire
I refused to evacuate from.
I lived in that charred shadow of a shelter.
I bled there, too.
Is it not love to give and give of oneself
until you become nothing more
than a bag of bones ground to powder
and mixed with the cement
patching up crumbling walls?

I told myself my ex loved me,
that black eyes were merely
his fist kissing my face with moon dust.
Anything can look pretty
if you drink enough.
Forgive me, liver,

for falling into that lie.
Forgive me, skin,
canvas battered with scars.

He had replaced me with a quiet mouth.
I am not perfect,
but I promise I won't love
like spontaneous combustion anymore.
I won't make myself disappear into silence
just so I can hear a whispered "I love you."

To anyone who says
they don't know what love is
supposed to feel like,
I say:
Me, too.

Dear Bullet

Dear Bullet,

It's been another rough day in America.
Another round of violence,
school children cowering under desks again.
The politicians keep telling me
it's too soon to demand an end
to this hemorrhaging of innocence.
So I come to you,
desperate hands raised to the sky
to prove I'm unarmed
except for the questions
I come ready to throw.

Dear Bullet,

How do I let Thoughts And Prayers
know I don't want to hear from them anymore?
How do we make our voices clearer
so money can't hold a candle
to the copper in our bleeding mouths?
I don't speak dollar signs.
I merely know that fear can be
the most paralyzing trauma.
I know what it's like
to find terror in safe spaces,
and I want it to stop.

Dear Bullet,

Jam, please,
and protest the objective
for which you were built.
School should never be funerals
blooming in a field of terror.
But here I find myself
begging a bullet for action
I can't seek from my own government.

Homegrown

Years ago my stepfather,
a white man with a well-manicured backyard,
planted a garden with the same enthusiasm
of a school child on the first day of summer.
These days that garden births tomatoes by the handful
and enough grapes to make gallons of wine in the basement.

My mother,
a white woman enjoying a glass of her husband's wine,
is sitting on the couch when a headline flashes across the TV
screen.
There's been a shooting.
Twelve people dead on a college campus.
The suspect in custody is described as a lone wolf,
a mentally ill former football star.
The suspect walks away in a bulletproof vest,
but the color of his pale skin
is the most effective protection from harm.

My mother changes the channel.
She will not call this an act of terrorism,
this daily bloodshed.
This is the same narrative as last year, last month, last week.
This is just the way things are in America.
Another shooting.
Rinse, repeat, go back to work.
Go back to sleep.

Ignore it all in the morning.
Drown out the next explosion of gunfire with a cup of coffee.
Ask your white friends how they're doing,
knowing full well the answer will be easy to swallow,
that they left home this morning
without wondering if they would make it back alive.

When I was twelve years old in September 2001
the adults in my white town
scrambled to help me make sense of things.
They kept saying "terrorism".
They kept saying "Muslim"
but they couldn't say Black Wall Street
or Timothy McVeigh and they definitely
wouldn't mention the KKK
because America refuses to talk about how
we create monsters ourselves.

This country has a terrorism problem,
but it is homegrown, not arriving from Syria or Iraq.
The skeletons in our closets are fortified by years of genocide.
They put on suits and play politician,
put on badges and become police officers.
The facades are endless.
So are the excuses.

Terrorism.
It looks like Confederate flags and tiki torches.
Polo shirts and weaponized vehicles.
It looks like a Bible study at a Black church
interrupted with gunfire.
A white hand on a trigger
in a Colorado movie theater.
A hotel room strewn with
high powered weapons in Las Vegas.
It looks like school children begging us to save them
so they can get an education.

Tomorrow this poem will contain outdated references
needing to be replaced with news of the next mass shooting.
Terrorists in America look like people we know.
The hoods are off and we're afraid to face them..
Too close for comfort.
Too familiar to be honest about.
We cannot fight a thing we refuse to name.

There is a mass shooting of 4 or more victims in the US
almost every single day.
But we don't call this a terrorism problem.

So when my stepfather starts thinking
about planting green beans,
he stands in the backyard surveying the options of the land.
He has no fear of what grows here.
He gives no thought to the young white men in his neighbor-
hood,
or how their hateful ideas might turn into shooting sprees.
He's too busy wondering if the sky might swell again
with hijacked airplanes
while his hands are covered in dirt.

Notes

All work is previously unpublished except for "The Alcoholic Considers Another Round" which appeared in *Words Dance,* "The Diagnosis (Runs In The Family)" which appeared in *Wicked Banshee Press*, and "Homegrown" which was anthologized in *RISE (An Anthology of Power and Unity)* by Vagabond Press.

Dylan Garcia (they/them) is a Best Of The Net nominated performance poet from Rockford, Illinois.

They have competed at the National Poetry Slam, the Individual World Poetry Slam, and were an individual finalist during the Rustbelt Regional Poetry Slam.

They can be found online as Dylan Garcia Poetry.

www.ingramcontent.com/pod-product-compliance
Lightning Source LLC
Chambersburg PA
CBHW031254130726
47988CB00008B/3350